Ev'ry Little Soul

Ev'ry Little Soul

Written by
Terry a. O'Neal

Illustrated by
Wendy Robinson

Motion Publications, P.O. Box 2551, Elk Grove, CA. 95624

Library of Congress Catalog Card Number
2002108951

ISBN # 0-9679446-6-X

Printed in Hong Kong

First Edition

10 9 8 7   6 5 4 3 2

To my children:

Michael Jr., Cameron, Latoya
&
Jorden Elizabeth

From mom
with lots of kisses and hugs

Come little children
barefoot and all,

young and old,
big and small.

Join hands together
gripped tight as chains.

United as one
from which we've come

on this earth

where we remain.

March!
Toy Soldiers
March!

Keep on moving
don't turn back,

it is weakness that you lackno force can tear you apart.

March!
Toy Soldiers
March!

One by one,
ev'ry little soul,

March!
Till you reach the sun.

Ev'ry Little Soul

Come little children
barefoot and all,

young and old
big and small.

Join hands together
gripped tight as chains.

United as one
from which we've come

on this earth
where we remain.

March!
Toy Soldiers
March!

Keep on moving
don't turn back,
it is weakness that you lackno force can tear you apart.

March!
Toy Soldiers
March!

One by one,
ev'ry little soul,
March!
Till you reach the sun.

MY TOY SOLDIERS

Michael Jr.   CAMERON   Jorden   L a t o y a

Terrance   Amyah   Khali

DeShawn   jAMiesHA

Ashley   Kaitlyn   Toshio

SAcorA   Debora   Leroy Jr.   Charmaine

Chantelle

Devonte

Jerry   T e v i n   Tenisha   NEKEIA

Micah   MARCUS

Leon III   SAMANTHA   A m a n d a

LaTavia   L e s l i e   Robert